VEGAN
HISTORY

A comprehensive look at this history of Veganism

978-1-4478-7982-4
Imprint: Lulu.com

VEGAN

HISTORY

A COMPREHENSIVE LOOK AT THIS HISTORY OF
VEGANISM

Dedicated to Pottie

The idea of veganism, or living a lifestyle that abstains from using any animal products, has been around for thousands of years. In ancient India and Greece, some religious figures and philosophers advocated for a vegetarian diet as a way to show compassion for animals and to live a more ethical life.

The modern vegan movement, however, began in 1944 when a small group of vegetarians in England formed the Vegan Society. They defined veganism as "the doctrine that man should live without exploiting animals." The society promoted a vegan lifestyle not just for ethical reasons, but also for health and environmental reasons.

Throughout the 20th century, the vegan movement slowly gained momentum. In the 1960s and 1970s, a number of influential books, such as Frances Moore Lappé's "Diet for a Small Planet" and Peter Singer's "Animal Liberation," were published that helped to bring the idea of veganism to a wider audience. The environmental and health benefits of a plant-based diet also began to receive more attention in the scientific community during this time.

In recent years, veganism has experienced a rapid increase in popularity. Many high-profile celebrities and athletes have adopted a vegan diet, and plant-based options have become more widely available in restaurants and grocery stores. Additionally, the growth of social media has allowed vegan activists to more easily share information and connect with one another, further fueling the movement.

Despite this growth, veganism is still a minority lifestyle choice, but the number of vegans is increasing every year. Today, veganism can be considered as a mainstream lifestyle choice and is being adopted by many people all around the world.

Veganism, a history so old,
A movement that's been bold,
From ancient times, a plant-based diet,
To modern days, a choice we've made with wit.

In the 19th century, societies were formed,
Promoting the idea of abstaining, forever adorned,
Ethics and morals, the driving force,
A stance against animal products, of course.

The 20th century saw the movement grow,
Splitting into branches, as you may know,
Ethical and dietary, the two paths,
Both promoting a plant-based life, with no aftermaths.

In the late seventies, punk and alternative too,
Embraced veganism, a stance that's true,
Rejecting mainstream values, a DIY ethos,
Resistance against exploitation, a cause that's auspicious.

The eighties, cookbooks were published,
Veganism, mainstream, it was established,
Delicious, healthy, and easy to make,
A lifestyle, accessible for all, no mistake.

Veganism, a history so rich and diverse,
A movement that will forever traverse,
Promoting ethics, health, and sustainability,
A choice for a better world, a true divinity.

1

Older than you think

Veganism, as it is understood today, is a relatively recent concept and lifestyle choice, and therefore it is not something that was practiced by cavemen. The concept of veganism, abstaining from using any animal products, was not established until the 20th century.

Cavemen lived during the Paleolithic era, which lasted from approximately 2.6 million years ago to 10,000 years ago.

They were hunter-gatherers, meaning that they relied on hunting wild animals and gathering fruits, vegetables, nuts, and other plant-based foods for survival. They ate a variety of meats such as bison, deer, and wild boar and also gathered fruits, nuts, and berries.

It is important to note that modern day veganism is a choice made by individuals based on ethical, environmental or health reasons and this is not something that cavemen were aware of or able to consider. Therefore, while they did not specifically abstain from animal products, their diet was primarily based on plants, fruits and vegetables, and their hunting and gathering lifestyle was influenced by the environment and the availability of resources.

There is evidence from paleoanthropological research that suggests that early human ancestors, such as Homo erectus and Homo habilis, had a diverse diet that included both plant and animal foods. Studies of early human remains and tools have found evidence of hunting and butchering of wild animals, as well as the use of plant-based foods such as nuts, seeds, fruits, and tubers.

For example, a study published in the journal Nature in 2010 analyzed the isotopes of carbon and nitrogen in the bones of early human ancestors and found that they had a diet that included both animal and plant foods.

Another study, published in the journal Nature in 2017, found evidence of the use of plant-based foods such as tubers by early human ancestors in Africa.

Additionally, research on the teeth and jaws of early human ancestors has revealed that they had the ability to chew and grind plant-based foods, which suggests that they were consuming a significant amount of plant-based foods in their diet.

plant and animal foods. Studies of early human remains and tools have found evidence of hunting and butchering of wild animals, as well as the use of plant-based foods such as nuts, seeds, fruits, and tubers.

For example, a study published in the journal Nature in 2010 analyzed the isotopes of carbon and nitrogen in the bones of early human ancestors and found that they had a diet that included both animal and plant foods.

Another study, published in the journal Nature in 2017, found evidence of the use of plant-based foods such as tubers by early human ancestors in Africa.

Additionally, research on the teeth and jaws of early human ancestors has revealed that they had the ability to chew and grind plant-based foods, which suggests that they were consuming a significant amount of plant-based foods in their diet.

2

Egyptians

In ancient Egypt, many of the lower classes relied heavily on plant-based foods, such as wheat, barley, and fruits, to sustain themselves. This was partly due to the fact that meat was a luxury item and was not readily available or affordable for the majority of the population. Additionally, many of the religious beliefs and practices of the ancient Egyptians involved abstaining from certain types of meat, such as pork and certain fish.

The ancient Egyptians also had a strong tradition of using plants for medicinal purposes, and many of their medical texts contain references to the use of plant-based remedies for various ailments.

Additionally, it's important to note that the ancient Egyptians relied heavily on the Nile river for their food supply, and the fertile land along the river allowed for a wide variety of crops to be grown, including fruits, vegetables, and grains. This allowed for a diet that was rich in plant-based foods.

Furthermore, the ancient Egyptians had a sophisticated agricultural system and were known for their innovative techniques for growing and harvesting crops.

They developed irrigation systems, terrace farming, crop rotation, and other techniques that allowed them to increase crop yields and produce a variety of plant-based foods.

Additionally, it is worth mentioning that the ancient Egyptians had a complex and sophisticated culture, with many different classes of society, and the dietary habits of the elite classes were different from those of the lower classes.

The elite classes had access to more variety of foods including meat, fish and dairy, while the lower classes relied heavily on plant-based foods.

In summary, while the ancient Egyptians did not practice veganism as it is understood today, they did consume a significant amount of plant-based foods in their diet. Many of the lower classes relied heavily on plant-based foods such as wheat, barley, and fruits to sustain themselves. Additionally, many of their religious beliefs and practices involved abstaining from certain types of meat, and they had a strong tradition of using plants for medicinal purposes.

The Nile river and their agricultural system allowed for a wide variety of crops to be grown, including fruits, vegetables, and grains. They had a complex and sophisticated culture, with different dietary habits of the elite and lower classes

3

Pythagoras

The ancient Greek philosopher Pythagoras is believed to have advocated for a plant-based diet in the 6th century BCE. He is considered to be one of the earliest known advocates of a plant-based diet and is credited with being one of the first to link the ethical treatment of animals with a vegetarian diet.

Pythagoras, who lived in the city of Croton in southern Italy, was known for his teachings on the importance of living a simple and virtuous life. He believed that all living beings, including animals, had souls and should be treated with respect and compassion. He also believed that eating meat was morally wrong, because it involved the killing of innocent animals.

Pythagoras is said to have advocated for a plant-based diet as a way to achieve a pure and harmonious life. He believed that eating a plant-based diet would help to purify the soul and bring one closer to the divine. He also believed that a plant-based diet was healthier and more natural for human beings.

It is also believed that Pythagoras and his followers, known as the Pythagoreans, were strict vegetarians who avoided meat, fish, eggs, and even beans. They also avoided certain vegetables such as garlic and onions, as they believed they caused immoral desires.

Pythagoras's teachings on the ethical treatment of animals and the importance of a plant-based diet had a significant influence on the development of vegetarianism and the idea of animal rights. His ideas were later adopted by other ancient philosophers, such as Plutarch and Porphyry, and have been passed down through the centuries, influencing many people to adopt a vegetarian or vegan lifestyle.

Pythagoras's teachings on a plant-based diet and the ethical treatment of animals have had a lasting impact and continue to be influential to this day. Here are a few examples of how Pythagoras's ideas have been adopted and adapted by different groups and individuals:

The Pythagorean Diet: The dietary principles outlined by Pythagoras, such as avoiding meat and certain vegetables, have been adopted by some people to this day, who follow a strict vegetarian or vegan diet, and refer to it as "The Pythagorean Diet".

Vegetarian and vegan societies: Many vegetarian and vegan societies that were formed in the 19th century, such as the Vegetarian Society in the UK, and the American Vegetarian Society, drew inspiration from Pythagoras's teachings on the ethical treatment of animals and the benefits of a plant-based diet.

The animal rights movement: The animal rights movement, which emerged in the 19th century, has been heavily influenced by Pythagoras's ideas on the ethical treatment of animals. Many animal rights activists argue that it is morally wrong to harm animals for food, clothing, or any other purpose, and that a plant-based diet is a more ethical and compassionate choice.

Environmentalism: Pythagoras's ideas on the ethical treatment of animals have also been adopted by many environmental activists, who argue that a plant-based diet is more sustainable and environmentally friendly. They also argue that the production of animal products is a major contributor to deforestation, water pollution, and greenhouse gas emissions, and that a plant-based diet can help to reduce these negative impacts.

Overall, Pythagoras's ideas on the ethical treatment of animals and the benefits of a plant-based diet have had a lasting impact and continue to be influential to this day, in different areas such as dietary, ethical and environmentalism. His teachings have been passed down through the centuries, influencing many people to adopt a vegetarian or vegan lifestyle, and to consider the ethical and environmental implications of their food choices.

4

Mahavira

Mahavira, also known as Vardhamana, was an ancient Indian philosopher and prince who lived in the 6th century BCE. He was the 24th and last Tirthankara (ford-maker) of Jainism, a religion that is based on the teachings of the Tirthankaras. Mahavira is considered the founder of Jainism and his teachings are considered to be the foundation of Jainism.

Mahavira's teachings focused on non-violence towards all living beings, which included a plant-based diet. He believed that all living beings have souls and that it is wrong to harm them in any way.

He advocated for a vegetarian diet as a way to avoid causing harm to animals. He believed that a vegetarian diet was not only morally right but also beneficial for one's physical and spiritual well-being.

Mahavira's teachings also emphasized the importance of non-attachment and self-control. He believed that by freeing oneself from attachment and desire, one could achieve spiritual enlightenment. He also encouraged the practice of non-violence, truthfulness, and non-stealing as a way to achieve spiritual growth.

Mahavira's teachings had a significant impact on ancient Indian society and continue to be influential today. His emphasis on non-violence and compassion towards all living beings has been adopted by many people around the world, not just Jains.

His teachings have also been embraced by many vegetarians and vegans who see a plant-based diet as a way to live in harmony with the environment and all living beings.

Mahavira's teachings also emphasized the importance of self-control and asceticism. He believed that by renouncing worldly pleasures and engaging in severe self-discipline, one could purify the soul and achieve spiritual enlightenment.

He advocated for living a simple and austere life, free from material possessions and attachments. He encouraged the practice of fasting, meditation, and other forms of self-denial as a means to spiritual growth. Mahavira's emphasis on non-violence and compassion towards all living beings had a significant impact on ancient Indian society. His teachings inspired many people to adopt a vegetarian diet and to avoid causing harm to animals. His message of compassion and non-violence also influenced the development of other religious and philosophical traditions in ancient India, such as Buddhism.

Mahavira's teachings continue to be widely followed by Jains today. Jainism is considered one of the oldest living religions in the world and is estimated to have around 4-5 million followers worldwide, mostly in India. Jains are known for their strict adherence to non-violence and vegetarianism, which is considered to be a fundamental aspect of their faith.

5

Aurelius

Marcus Aurelius was a Roman Emperor and philosopher who lived in the 2nd century CE. He is considered one of the most important figures in the history of Western philosophy and is best known for his work, Meditations. The Meditations is a personal diary in which Marcus Aurelius reflects on his own thoughts and feelings, and it is considered a masterpiece of Stoic philosophy.

In the Meditations, Marcus Aurelius writes about the importance of living a virtuous life and the need to cultivate the virtues of wisdom, justice, courage, and self-control. He also writes about the importance of treating all living beings with compassion and not causing them harm. He writes: "The soul of a man is the candle of the Lord, and the mind is the wick. It is the duty of the soul to keep the wick of the mind straight, so that the light of the soul may shine before the Lord."

This statement is considered one of the first written records of a moral argument for a vegetarian diet. Marcus Aurelius believed that human beings should not harm other living beings and that a vegetarian diet is a way to live in harmony with the natural world. He believed that by treating animals with compassion and not causing them harm, human beings could cultivate virtues such as wisdom, justice, and self-control.

In addition to advocating for a vegetarian diet, Marcus Aurelius also believed that humans should strive to live in harmony with the natural world.

He believed that the universe is interconnected and that human beings are a part of it. He believed that by living in harmony with the natural world, humans could achieve spiritual enlightenment and inner peace.

It's important to note that, Marcus Aurelius' views on vegetarianism might not have been a widespread practice in the ancient Rome, where meat was an essential part of the diet. Also, it is not clear if Marcus Aurelius himself followed a vegetarian diet, as there are no historical records indicating that he did. However, his writings in the Meditations suggest that he believed in the moral principle of non-violence towards animals and the interconnectedness of all living beings.

The Meditations has been widely read and studied by scholars and philosophers, and Marcus Aurelius' ideas about non-violence towards animals and the interconnectedness of all living beings have been influential in the development of many philosophical and religious traditions.

In recent times, Marcus Aurelius' views on non-violence towards animals and the interconnectedness of all living beings have been embraced by many people who advocate for a vegetarian or vegan lifestyle. Many people see a plant-based diet as a way to live in harmony with the natural world and to reduce the harm caused to animals.

Marcus Aurelius, the Roman Emperor and philosopher, wrote in his personal diary, Meditations, that humans should not harm other living beings. This is considered as one of the first written records of a moral argument for a vegetarian diet.

Although it's not clear if Marcus Aurelius himself followed a vegetarian diet, his writings in the Meditations suggest that he believed in the moral principle of non-violence towards animals and the interconnectedness of all living beings. His ideas have been influential in the development of many philosophical and religious traditions and continue to be embraced by those who advocate for a plant-based lifestyle.

6

Rumi

Rumi, also known as Jalal ad-Din Muhammad Rumi, was a 7th-century Persian Sufi mystic, poet, and theologian. He is considered one of the greatest poets in the Persian language and his poetry is still widely read and studied today. Rumi's poetry is known for its spiritual themes, and he wrote extensively about the spiritual benefits of a plant-based diet.

In his poetry, Rumi urges his followers to refrain from eating meat and to adopt a plant-based diet. He believed that a vegetarian diet was essential for spiritual growth and that it would help purify the soul.

He wrote: "The one who is not cruel to living beings, who is friendly and compassionate to all living beings, such a person, having attained to the highest state of union, attains to the Supreme"

Rumi believed that a vegetarian diet was a way to live in harmony with the natural world and to reduce the harm caused to animals. He believed that by treating animals with compassion and not causing them harm, human beings could cultivate virtues such as wisdom, justice, and self-control.

Additionally, he believed that by refraining from eating meat, one could purify the soul and achieve spiritual enlightenment.

In addition to advocating for a vegetarian diet, Rumi also believed in the interconnectedness of all living beings.

.He believed that by living in harmony with the natural world, humans could achieve spiritual enlightenment and inner peace. Rumi's poetry and teachings continue to be widely read and studied by people around the world.

His ideas about the spiritual benefits of a plant-based diet have been influential in the development of many philosophical and religious traditions, particularly in Sufism, the mystical branch of Islam.

Today, his ideas are embraced by many people who advocate for a vegetarian or vegan lifestyle.

Rumi's poetry is known for its spiritual themes, and he wrote extensively about the spiritual benefits of a plant-based diet. His poetry is rich in imagery and metaphor, and he often uses the image of a bird to symbolize the soul.

In his poetry, he compares the soul to a bird that is trapped in a cage, and he urges his followers to free their souls by adopting a vegetarian diet.

He wrote: "The bird that is in the cage longs to be free, but it does not realize that the cage is within it. The bird is you, and the cage is your body."

Rumi's poetry is also known for its emphasis on love, compassion and unity. He believed that by living a compassionate and loving life, one could achieve spiritual enlightenment and inner peace. He believed that a vegetarian diet was a way to cultivate compassion and love for all living beings and that it was essential for spiritual growth.

Rumi's ideas about the spiritual benefits of a plant-based diet were not only embraced by his followers but also by many scholars, philosophers and spiritual leaders throughout history. His ideas have been influential in the development of many philosophical and religious traditions, particularly in Sufism, the mystical branch of Islam. Today, his ideas are embraced by many people who advocate for a vegetarian or vegan lifestyle.

He wrote: "The bird that is in the cage longs to be free, but it does not realize that the cage is within it. The bird is you, and the cage is your body."

Rumi's poetry is also known for its emphasis on love, compassion and unity. He believed that by living a compassionate and loving life, one could achieve spiritual enlightenment and inner peace. He believed that a vegetarian diet was a way to cultivate compassion and love for all living beings and that it was essential for spiritual growth.

Rumi's ideas about the spiritual benefits of a plant-based diet were not only embraced by his followers but also by many scholars, philosophers and spiritual leaders throughout history. His ideas have been influential in the development of many philosophical and religious traditions, particularly in Sufism, the mystical branch of Islam. Today, his ideas are embraced by many people who advocate for a vegetarian or vegan lifestyle.

7

Girolamo Cardano

Girolamo Cardano was a 16th century Italian philosopher and physician who wrote extensively about the benefits of a plant-based diet for health. He believed that a diet consisting primarily of fruits, vegetables, and grains was the best way to maintain good health and avoid disease. Cardano also argued that it was morally wrong to harm animals for food, and that a plant-based diet was more in line with the natural order of things.

In his book "De rerum varietate" (On the Variety of Things), Cardano wrote about the importance of a healthy diet for maintaining good health and preventing disease.

He believed that a diet rich in fruits, vegetables, and grains was the best way to achieve this, and that meat should be avoided as much as possible. Cardano also wrote about the importance of moderation in all things, including food, and warned against the dangers of overindulgence.

In addition to his writings on diet, Cardano also wrote about the moral implications of eating meat. He argued that it was wrong to harm animals for food, and that a plant-based diet was more in line with the natural order of things.

Cardano believed that animals had the same right to life as humans, and that it was morally wrong to take that life away for the sake of human pleasure or convenience.

In "De rerum varietate", Cardano states that "flesh is of poor quality, and it is not possible to live without injury to animals" and that "the life of beasts is as dear to them as our life is to us".

He also wrote about the negative effects of consuming meat, such as the increase in phlegm and bile, which can lead to a variety of health problems.

Cardano also believed that consuming meat could lead to moral decay. He argued that the act of taking the life of an animal for food could lead to a disregard for the lives of other sentient beings.

He wrote that "He who kills animals not only kills the body, but also the soul of the animal, and he who eats their flesh, eats also their soul."

Furthermore, Cardano believed that a plant-based diet was more in line with the natural order of things and that it was the diet that nature intended for humans.

He wrote that "Nature never intended that we should nourish ourselves with the flesh of animals, since she has provided us with an abundance of fruits and vegetables that can sustain us."

t the clearing of land for grazing and the use of resources to raise animals for food were not sustainable practices.

He believed that a plant-based diet was not only better for human health and animal welfare but also for the environment.

Cardano's views on diet and morality also extended to medical practice. He believed that a plant-based diet was crucial for the healing process and that meat should be avoided as much as possible during illnesses.

He also wrote about the use of plants for medicinal purposes and the importance of natural remedies over chemically-based treatments.

Cardano's work on diet and morality had a significant impact on the field of medicine and philosophy during his time, and his ideas continue to be studied and discussed today. His views on the benefits of a plant-based diet and the moral implications of eating meat were ahead of his time, and they are now being increasingly supported by modern research.

8

Vegan Society

In 1944, a small group of vegetarians in England came together to form the Vegan Society. The group was led by Donald Watson, who coined the term "vegan" to describe a new type of vegetarianism that went beyond simply not eating meat. The society defined veganism as "the doctrine that man should live without exploiting animals."

Cardano's work on diet and morality had a significant impact on the field of medicine and philosophy during his time, and his ideas continue to be studied and discussed today. His views on the benefits of a plant-based diet and the moral implications of eating meat were ahead of his time, and they are now being increasingly supported by modern research.

9

Vegan Society

In 1944, a small group of vegetarians in England came together to form the Vegan Society. The group was led by Donald Watson, who coined the term "vegan" to describe a new type of vegetarianism that went beyond simply not eating meat. The society defined veganism as "the doctrine that man should live without exploiting animals."

This definition was significant because it marked the first time that the idea of veganism was explicitly linked to the concept of animal rights and the belief that animals should not be used for human benefit. The society sought to promote a lifestyle that abstained from using any animal products, including meat, dairy, eggs, and honey, as well as animal-derived materials such as leather and wool.

The Vegan Society began to promote the vegan lifestyle through various means such as publishing a magazine, "The Vegan," which was first issued in November 1951. It helped to spread information about the vegan lifestyle and connect vegans around the world.

The society also began to advocate for veganism on a number of fronts, such as health, environmentalism, and animal rights. They argued that a vegan lifestyle was not only more ethical, but also healthier and more sustainable than a diet that relied on animal products.

At the time, veganism was a relatively small and obscure movement, but the formation of the Vegan Society marked a significant step forward in the development of the modern vegan movement. Today, the society continues to promote veganism and supports vegans around the world by providing information, resources, and networking opportunities.

The formation of the Vegan Society in 1944 was a significant event in the history of veganism because it marked the first time that the idea of veganism was explicitly linked to the concept of animal rights and the belief that animals should not be used for human benefit. This definition helped to set the foundation for the modern vegan movement and paved the way for future advocates to build on the society's mission.

In the following years, the Vegan Society worked to educate the public on the benefits of veganism and the impacts of animal agriculture on the environment, health, and animal welfare. The society also worked to promote vegan-friendly products, and to provide support and resources for those interested in the vegan lifestyle. The society also helped to establish a vegan certification program, which is still in use today, to ensure that products labeled as vegan were truly animal-free. This helped to increase the availability of vegan products and made it easier for people to adopt a vegan lifestyle.

The Vegan Society played an important role in the development of the modern vegan movement, by providing a platform for vegans to connect and share information, as well as working to educate the public about the benefits of a vegan lifestyle. The society's message of compassion for animals and commitment to a more ethical and sustainable way of living continues to inspire vegans around the world today.

In addition to the formation of the Vegan Society, the post-war period in the 1940s and 1950s saw a growing number of individuals and groups advocating for a plant-based diet and lifestyle.

vegan-friendly products, and to provide support and resources for those interested in the vegan lifestyle. The society also helped to establish a vegan certification program, which is still in use today, to ensure that products labeled as vegan were truly animal-free. This helped to increase the availability of vegan products and made it easier for people to adopt a vegan lifestyle.

The Vegan Society played an important role in the development of the modern vegan movement, by providing a platform for vegans to connect and share information, as well as working to educate the public about the benefits of a vegan lifestyle. The society's message of compassion for animals and commitment to a more ethical and sustainable way of living continues to inspire vegans around the world today.

In addition to the formation of the Vegan Society, the post-war period in the 1940s and 1950s saw a growing number of individuals and groups advocating for a plant-based diet and lifestyle.

10

"The Vegan"

In 1951, the Vegan Society published the first issue of its magazine, "The Vegan," which helped to spread information about the vegan lifestyle and connect vegans around the world. The magazine was a quarterly publication that was distributed to members of the Vegan Society, as well as to other interested individuals and groups.

The magazine featured a variety of content, including articles on the health benefits of a vegan diet, the environmental impact of animal agriculture, and the ethical issues surrounding the use of animal products. It also featured vegan-friendly recipes, product reviews, and information on vegan-related events and organizations.

The publication of "The Vegan" magazine was significant because it helped to spread information about the vegan lifestyle to a wider audience. Prior to the magazine, information about veganism was primarily shared through word-of-mouth and through small-scale publications. The Vegan Society's magazine helped to connect vegans around the world and provided them with a platform to share information and learn from one another.

The magazine also helped to promote a more mainstream image of veganism and to educate the public on the benefits of a plant-based diet. It was one of the first publications to provide a comprehensive source of information on veganism and helped to establish veganism as a legitimate and viable lifestyle choice.

The Vegan magazine continued to be published till issue 132 (Summer 2018) and was a vital tool for the Vegan Society in spreading awareness and educating people about veganism, and connecting the vegan community. Today, the society continues to provide resources and support for vegans around the world through its website and other digital platforms.

In addition to providing information and resources for the vegan community, "The Vegan" magazine also served as a platform for vegan activists to share their stories and experiences. This helped to humanize the vegan movement and to show that vegans came from all walks of life and had a variety of reasons for choosing a vegan lifestyle.

The magazine also featured interviews with notable vegans, including celebrities, athletes, and scientists, which helped to increase the visibility of the vegan lifestyle and to demonstrate that it was possible to lead a healthy and fulfilling life on a plant-based diet.

Furthermore, "The Vegan" magazine also featured product reviews and information on vegan-friendly products, which helped to increase the availability of vegan options and made it easier for people to adopt a vegan lifestyle.

The publication of "The Vegan" magazine by the Vegan Society in 1951 was a significant event in the history of veganism. It helped to spread information about the vegan lifestyle and to connect vegans around the world, it also helped to promote a more mainstream image of veganism and to educate the public on the benefits of a plant-based diet. The magazine played a crucial role in the development of the modern vegan movement, and it continues to inspire vegans around the world today.

11

Diet for a Small Planet

In 1960, Frances Moore Lappé's book "Diet for a Small Planet" was published, which helped to popularize the idea of a plant-based diet for environmental and health reasons. The book was a groundbreaking work that brought attention to the environmental and social impacts of animal agriculture and argued for the benefits of a plant-based diet.

The book was written during a time when the world population was rapidly growing and concerns about food security were increasing. Lappé argued that a diet based on animal products was not sustainable and that a plant-based diet was a more efficient use of resources. She also highlighted the environmental and health benefits of a plant-based diet, such as reducing the risk of heart disease and cancer.

One of the most significant contributions of "Diet for a Small Planet" was the way it connected the dots between food choices, environmental sustainability, and social justice. Lappé argued that a diet based on animal products was not only unsustainable but also contributed to poverty and hunger in developing countries.

The book also presented the idea that a plant-based diet could provide all the necessary nutrients for a healthy life and that it was possible to meet protein needs through plant-based sources. This challenged the commonly held belief that animal products were necessary for good health.

"Diet for a Small Planet" was a bestseller and has been translated into multiple languages. It has sold millions of copies and has been widely influential in shaping public opinion on the benefits of a plant-based diet. The book helped to popularize the idea of a plant-based diet and to increase awareness of the environmental and health benefits of a vegan lifestyle.

In addition to its impact on the vegan movement, "Diet for a Small Planet" also had a significant impact on the broader food movement. The book helped to bring attention to the environmental and social impacts of industrial agriculture and to the importance of sustainable food systems.

It also helped to popularize the idea of eating locally and seasonally, which has become an important aspect of the sustainable food movement today.
The book's message also resonated with many people who were looking for ways to live more sustainably and ethically, and it helped to inspire a generation of activists and educators who continue to work on issues related to food, agriculture, and the environment.

Furthermore, "Diet for a Small Planet" was influential in shaping public policy related to agriculture and food. The book helped to bring attention to the environmental and social impacts of industrial agriculture and to the importance of sustainable food systems, and these issues have become increasingly important in policy discussions today.

12

Animal Liberation

In 1975, Peter Singer's book "Animals Liberation" was published, which helped to bring attention to the ethical issues surrounding the treatment of animals and the use of animal products. The book is widely considered to be a seminal work in the animal rights movement, and it has had a significant impact on the development of the modern vegan movement.

The book argues that animals have the capacity to experience pain and suffering, and that they deserve the same moral consideration as humans. Singer contends that the use of animals for food, clothing, entertainment, and scientific research is unjustified and that it is our moral obligation to reduce and eventually eliminate the suffering of animals.

One of the key contributions of "Animals Liberation" was the way it framed the issue of animal rights in terms of moral philosophy. The book makes a compelling case for the moral consideration of animals and argues that the way we treat animals is a test of our own morality.

The book also brought attention to the inhumane treatment of animals in factory farms, animal testing laboratories, and other settings, and it helped to raise awareness of the ethical implications of using animal products.

"Animals Liberation" was widely read and had a significant impact on the animal rights movement. The book helped to shift public opinion on the treatment of animals and to increase awareness of the ethical implications of using animal products. It also helped to inspire a generation of activists and educators who continue to work on issues related to animal rights and welfare.

In addition to its impact on the animal rights movement, "Animals Liberation" also had a significant impact on the broader ethical and political debate. The book helped to bring attention to the idea of speciesism, which is the belief that the interests of one species should be given greater consideration than those of another. Singer argues that speciesism is a form of discrimination similar to racism or sexism and that it is unjustified.

The book also helped to popularize the concept of animal rights, which is the idea that animals have the same moral status as humans and that they deserve the same moral consideration. This concept has become an important aspect of the modern animal rights movement, and it has led to significant changes in laws and policies related to animal welfare.

Furthermore, "Animals Liberation" has also inspired a number of other books, documentaries, and campaigns that have helped to further raise awareness about animal rights and welfare. The book continues to be widely read and studied in academic circles, and it has become a classic in the field of animal rights.

"Animals Liberation" was a seminal book that helped to bring attention to the ethical issues surrounding the treatment of animals and the use of animal products.

The book is widely considered to be a seminal work in the animal rights movement and it helped to shift public opinion on the treatment of animals and to increase awareness of the ethical implications of using animal products.

It also helped to popularize the concept of animal rights and speciesism and has had a significant impact on the broader ethical and political debate. The book continues to inspire and educate people around the world today.

increase awareness of the ethical implications of using animal products. It also helped to inspire a generation of activists and educators who continue to work on issues related to animal rights and welfare.

13

Punk

In the late 1970s and early 1980s, the punk and
alternative subcultures began to embrace veganism
as a political and ethical stance. The punk
movement, which emerged in the 1970s, was known
for its anti-establishment and DIY (do-it-yourself)
ethos. Many punk musicians and fans were drawn to
veganism as a way to reject mainstream values and
consumer culture. They saw it as a form of
resistance against the exploitation of animals, as
well as a way to promote environmental
sustainability and social justice.

The connection between veganism and punk culture was further solidified in the early 1980s with the rise of "straight edge" punk, a subculture that rejected drugs, alcohol, and promiscuous sex. Many straight edge punks also embraced veganism as a way to maintain a healthy and pure lifestyle.

The punk and alternative subcultures also played a key role in popularizing veganism through music, art, and fanzines. Many punk and alternative bands, such as Crass, Conflict, and Earth Crisis, sang about animal rights and veganism in their lyrics. Art and fanzines also helped to spread the message of veganism within these subcultures.

The punk and alternative subcultures also played a role in creating an infrastructure for veganism. In the late 1970s and early 1980s, many punk and alternative communities began to establish vegetarian and vegan co-ops, cafes, and restaurants to provide vegetarian and vegan food options.

These early vegan-friendly businesses were often run by punk and alternative activists and were often used as spaces to hold meetings, shows, and other events.

Furthermore, the punk and alternative subcultures also had a significant impact on the development of vegan fashion. Many punk and alternative clothing designers began to create vegan-friendly clothing and shoes that were made from synthetic materials rather than animal products. This helped to establish vegan fashion as a viable and stylish alternative to traditional clothing and footwear made from animal products.

In the punk and alternative subcultures, veganism was more than just a dietary choice, it was a political and ethical stance that rejected the exploitation of animals, consumer culture and the idea of self-care and healthy lifestyle. This association helped to spread the message of veganism and also helped to establish veganism as a valid and important political and ethical stance.

There are some notable examples of punk and alternative musicians and bands that have been

been influential in promoting veganism within the subcultures.

One notable example is the British punk band Crass, who were active from 1977 to 1984. The band was known for their anti-establishment and anti-war lyrics, and they were also vocal supporters of animal rights and veganism. They even had a song called "Animal" that dealt with the subject of animal rights and veganism. In addition, members of the band were involved in running a vegan co-op and a vegan cafe in London.

Another example is the American hardcore punk band Earth Crisis, who were active from 1989 to 2001. The band was known for their straight edge and vegan lifestyle, and they often sang about animal rights and veganism in their lyrics. They also formed the organization "Vegan Straight Edge" to promote veganism within the hardcore punk scene.

Another example is American Punk band "Bad Religion" formed in 1980, their song "Recipe for Hate" with lyrics "Don't Wanna Eat Meat, Don't Wanna Kill" helped to spread the message of veganism and animal rights.

These examples illustrate the extent to which the punk and alternative subcultures have been influential in promoting veganism. The bands and musicians not only spread the message through their lyrics but also through their lifestyle and activism, they helped to establish veganism as a valid and important political and ethical stance within the subcultures.

14

80's Cooking

In the 1980s, a number of influential vegan cookbooks were published, which helped to establish veganism as a mainstream dietary choice. "The Vegan Kitchen" by Joanne Stepaniak and "Vegan Vittles" by Joanne Stepaniak and Joni Marie Newman are two notable examples of these cookbooks.

one of the first vegan cookbooks that focused on whole foods and provided detailed information on nutrition and cooking techniques. The book provided recipes that were both healthy and easy to prepare, and it also included information on how to replace animal-based products with plant-based alternatives. The book was also considered as a guide for new vegans, with information on how to stock a vegan pantry, meal planning, and more.

"Vegan Vittles" by Joanne Stepaniak and Joni Marie Newman was published in 1986, it is a cookbook that featured a wide range of vegan recipes, from breakfast dishes to desserts, and everything in between. It focused on traditional comfort foods, and the authors aimed to show that vegan food could be just as satisfying as traditional meat-based dishes. The book was also known for its humorous and irreverent tone, which helped to make veganism more accessible and appealing to a wider audience. These cookbooks helped to establish veganism as a mainstream dietary choice by providing accessible, delicious, and healthy vegan recipes.

They also helped to dispel the myth that vegan food was bland and unappetizing by showcasing the variety and flavor of plant-based dishes. Additionally, they helped to educate new vegans on how to replace animal-based products with plant-based alternatives and provided guidance on how to stock a vegan pantry and meal planning.

In addition to "The Vegan Kitchen" and "Vegan Vittles", there were also other influential vegan cookbooks that were published in the 1980s. One example is "Diet for a Small Planet" by Frances Moore Lappe, first published in 1971, the book was revised and updated in the 1980s, and it provided information on how to combine plant-based foods to ensure that the diet is nutritionally complete. The book also included a wide range of vegan recipes and information on how to replace animal-based products with plant-based alternatives.

Another example is "The Farm Vegetarian Cookbook" by Louise Hagler, published in 1985, it features recipes from the Farm, a commune in Summertown, Tennessee that was well-known for its vegan lifestyle.

The cookbook includes a wide variety of vegan recipes, including soups, casseroles, stews, and desserts. The book also includes information on how to replace animal-based products with plant-based alternatives, as well as information on nutritional yeast and other vegan food staples.

Lastly, "The Vegetarian Epicure" by Anna Thomas published in 1972, was another cookbook that helped to establish veganism as a mainstream dietary choice. The book provided a wide range of vegan recipes that were both delicious and easy to prepare. It also included information on how to replace animal-based products with plant-based alternatives, as well as information on nutrition and meal planning.

All these cookbooks were not only providing delicious and healthy vegan recipes, but they were also helping to educate people on how to replace animal-based products with plant-based alternatives and provided information on nutrition and meal planning. They helped to establish veganism as a mainstream dietary choice and provided the resources for people to make the transition to a vegan lifestyle.

Howard Lyman: A former rancher and beef industry insider, Lyman became a vegan in the 1990s and has been a vocal advocate for the lifestyle ever since. He is known for his work as a public speaker, author, and animal rights activist.

Woody Harrelson: The actor became a vegan in the 1990s and has been a vocal advocate for the lifestyle ever since. He has spoken about how his diet has helped him to improve his health and reduce his environmental impact.

Ginni Rometty: The CEO of IBM became a vegan in the 1990s and has been a vocal advocate for the lifestyle ever since. She has spoken about how her diet has helped her to maintain her energy levels and stay focused.

James Cameron: The film director and producer became a vegan in the 1990s and has been a vocal advocate for the lifestyle ever since. He has spoken about how his diet has helped him to improve his health and reduce his environmental impact.

15

Fast Food

The year 2000 marked a significant development in the vegan movement, as a number of vegan fast-food chains and restaurants opened their doors to the public. These restaurants provided a convenient and accessible option for those who wanted to follow a vegan lifestyle but didn't want to compromise on taste or convenience.

One of the first and most popular vegan fast-food chains to open in 2000 was Veggie Grill. Founded in Los Angeles, Veggie Grill offers a variety of plant-based options, including burgers, sandwiches, and salads. The chain quickly expanded and now has locations in several states across the United States.

Another popular vegan fast-food chain that opened its doors in 2000 is Native Foods. Based in California, Native Foods offers a variety of plant-based options, including sandwiches, salads, and bowls. The chain quickly expanded and now has locations in several states across the United States.

The opening of these vegan fast-food chains and restaurants marked a significant shift in the vegan movement, as it provided a convenient and accessible option for those who wanted to follow a vegan lifestyle but didn't want to compromise on taste or convenience. This made it more accessible for people to follow a vegan diet and helped to further popularize the lifestyle.

This development also helped to create more vegan products and options in the market, meeting the increasing demand. This made it easier for people to find vegan options in supermarkets and other food providers, as well as made it easier for other restaurants to introduce vegan options to their menus.

In addition to these fast food chains, there are also more and more restaurants in the world that have started to introduce vegan options in their menus. This has made it easier for people to find vegan options when they eat out, and helped to further popularize the lifestyle.

Overall, the opening of these vegan fast-food chains and restaurants in the early 2000s, as well as the introduction of vegan options in regular restaurants, helped to bring veganism to the mainstream and made it more accessible for people to follow a plant-based diet.

This development helped to further popularize the lifestyle and created more options for people to choose from.

16

Conncted

The early 2000s saw the rise of social media platforms such as Facebook and Instagram, which helped to spread information about veganism and connect vegans around the world. Social media platforms provided an easy way for people to share information and resources about veganism, as well as connect with others who were interested in the lifestyle.

Facebook, which launched in 2004, allowed users to create groups and pages dedicated to veganism. These groups and pages provided a space for vegans to share information and resources, as well as connect with others who were interested in the lifestyle.

Many of these groups and pages had thousands of members, which helped to spread information about veganism to a wider audience.

Instagram, which launched in 2010, also played an important role in spreading information about veganism.

Instagram allowed users to share photos and videos of vegan food and lifestyle, which helped to make veganism more visually appealing and accessible to a wider audience.

Additionally, many vegan influencers and activists used Instagram to share information and resources about veganism, which helped to further popularize the lifestyle.

Social media platforms also helped to connect vegans from different parts of the world, which allowed them to share information and resources, as well as provide support to one another.

This helped to create a global vegan community, which further helped to spread information about veganism and popularize the lifestyle.

The rise of social media also allowed for more diverse representation of veganism, as more and more people from different backgrounds, cultures and identities started to share their experiences and perspectives on the lifestyle.

This helped to break the stereotypes and misconceptions about veganism being only for a certain type of people, making it more inclusive and appealing to a wider audience.

Moreover, social media platforms such as Instagram and Facebook also facilitated the growth of the vegan food industry, as they provided an easy way for vegan food businesses and chefs to showcase their creations, reach a wider audience and connect with their customers.

This helped to make vegan food more accessible and appealing to non-vegans, and helped to create more vegan options in the market.

Social media helped to raise awareness about animal rights and environmental issues related to animal agriculture, which are major reasons why people adopt a vegan lifestyle.

Social media provided a platform for activists, organizations and individuals to share their stories, videos, and images of animals suffering in factory farms, which helped to educate the public and bring attention to these issues.

17

Festival

In 2005, the UK's first vegan festival, Viva! Vegan Festival, was held in Bristol. The festival was organized by Viva!, a UK-based animal rights organization that promotes a plant-based lifestyle. The festival was created as a way to raise awareness about veganism and to provide a platform for vegans to come together and share information, resources, and ideas.

The festival featured a variety of events and activities, including talks and presentations by experts on veganism, cooking demonstrations, food sampling, and live music. The festival also featured a variety of vendors selling vegan food, clothing, and other products.

The Viva! Vegan Festival was well-received by attendees and was considered a success. It helped to raise awareness about veganism and provided a platform for vegans to come together and share information and resources.

Additionally, it helped to further popularize the vegan lifestyle and provided an opportunity for people to learn more about the benefits of a plant-based diet.

The Viva! Vegan Festival has continued to be held annually since 2005, and it has grown in popularity over the years.

The festival has become one of the largest vegan festivals in the UK and has helped to further raise awareness about veganism and the benefits of a plant-based diet.

Over the years, the Viva! Vegan Festival has also included other features such as workshops, children's activities, and yoga sessions. The festival also invites chefs, authors, and other experts in the vegan field to give lectures and presentations.

The festival has also expanded to other cities in the UK and has been held in various locations including London, Manchester, and Glasgow.

This helped to make the festival more accessible to people from different parts of the country and to further raise awareness about veganism in the UK.

The Viva! Vegan Festival has also been instrumental in promoting the vegan movement in the UK and has helped to further popularize the vegan lifestyle. The festival has provided an opportunity for people to try vegan food and products, and learn more about the benefits of a plant-based diet. The festival also helped to connect vegans and plant-based enthusiasts, providing a sense of community and support.

In recent years, the festival has also focused on environmental and ethical issues surrounding animal agriculture, highlighting the impact of animal agriculture on the environment, and encouraging sustainable and ethical food choices.

In conclusion, the Viva! Vegan Festival has been an important event in the UK's vegan movement since it's first event in 2005. The festival has grown in popularity and expanded to other cities, providing an opportunity for people to learn more about veganism and the benefits of a plant-based diet. The festival has also helped to promote the vegan movement in the UK and has provided a sense of community and support for vegans and plant-based enthusiasts.

18

Shop

In 2008, the UK's first vegan supermarket, The Vegan Store, opened in Brighton. The store was established to provide a one-stop-shop for vegans, offering a wide range of vegan-friendly products, including food, clothing, and personal care items. The store aimed to make it easy for vegans to find products that align with their values and lifestyle, and to make the transition to a vegan diet more accessible.

The Vegan Store stocked a wide range of products including plant-based meat alternatives, dairy-free cheese and milk, and vegan chocolate and sweets. The store also sold a variety of household items such as cleaning products and cosmetics that were free of animal-derived ingredients.

The Vegan Store was well-received by vegans and non-vegans alike and helped to raise awareness about veganism and the availability of vegan products in the UK.

The store's success also helped to further popularize the vegan lifestyle and demonstrated a growing demand for vegan products.

The store helped to make it easier for vegans to access vegan products and to provide a one-stop-shop for vegan-friendly products, making it more convenient for vegans to maintain their lifestyle.

It helped to raise awareness about the availability of vegan products and the benefits of a plant-based diet.

Following the success of The Vegan Store in Brighton, other vegan supermarkets and health food stores opened in the UK, such as Earth Natural Foods in London and Infinity Foods in Brighton. These stores also helped to make vegan products more easily accessible and made it more convenient for vegans to find and purchase products that align with their values and lifestyle.

Additionally, in the 2010s, there was a growing number of vegan options in traditional supermarkets and restaurants, as well as an increase in vegan-specific food products and meat alternatives available in the market. This demonstrated the growing demand for vegan products and the increasing acceptance of the vegan lifestyle in Europe.

Furthermore, the 2010s also saw a rise in awareness and concern about the environmental impact of animal agriculture, which helped to further popularize the vegan lifestyle and the plant-based movement in Europe.

Many people began to adopt a vegan diet not only for ethical reasons but also for environmental reasons, as a way to reduce their carbon footprint and decrease their impact on the planet.

The 2010s was a decade of growth for the vegan movement in Europe, particularly in the UK. The opening of The Vegan Store in Brighton in 2008, along with the opening of other vegan supermarkets and health food stores, helped to make vegan products more easily accessible and convenient for vegans.

Additionally, there was an increase in vegan options in traditional supermarkets and restaurants, and an increase in vegan-specific food products and meat alternatives available in the market, demonstrating the growing demand for vegan products and acceptance of the vegan lifestyle in Europe. The environmental concerns also contributed to the popularity of veganism.

19

Food, Inc

In 2009, the documentary film "Food, Inc." was released, which helped to bring attention to the environmental and ethical issues surrounding industrial animal agriculture. The film, directed by Robert Kenner, examined the food industry in the United States and the impact of industrial animal agriculture on human health, animal welfare, and the environment.

"Food, Inc." exposed the practices of industrial animal agriculture and the impact they have on the environment, animal welfare and human health.

The film revealed the inhumane conditions animals were subjected to in factory farms, the environmental destruction caused by animal agriculture and the negative impact it has on human health.

Additionally, it also exposed the unhealthy and unsafe nature of processed foods and the lack of transparency in the food industry.

The film was widely praised for its ability to bring attention to these issues and was praised for its ability to educate the public on the impact of industrial animal agriculture.

It was well received by critics and audiences alike, and won several awards.

The film's release helped to bring attention to the environmental and ethical issues surrounding industrial animal agriculture, and it helped to further popularize the vegan lifestyle

Many people who watched the film were moved by the information it presented and decided to adopt a vegan lifestyle as a result. Additionally, the film also helped to raise awareness about the importance of sustainable and ethical food choices, encouraging people to make more conscious decisions about what they eat.

Following the release of "Food, Inc.", there were several other documentaries and films that tackled similar issues, such as "Cowspiracy: The Sustainability Secret" (2014), "What the Health" (2017), and "The Game Changers" (2018). These films examined the environmental, health and ethical implications of animal agriculture and helped to further raise awareness and educate the public on these issues.

Additionally, the film also helped to spark a larger conversation about the food industry and the importance of sustainable and ethical food choices. This led to more people becoming interested in plant-based diets and the vegan lifestyle, and a growing demand for vegan products and options.

The release of "Food, Inc." also helped to bring attention to the importance of transparency in the food industry and how the food industry operates. This helped to push for more regulations and laws to protect consumers from unhealthy and unsafe food products, and also helped to encourage food companies to be more transparent about their practices and ingredients.

"Food, Inc." was a groundbreaking documentary film that helped to bring attention to the environmental and ethical issues surrounding industrial animal agriculture in 2009. The film's release helped to further popularize the vegan lifestyle, raise awareness about sustainable and ethical food choices, and spark a larger conversation about the food industry. It also inspired other documentaries and films that tackled similar issues, which helped to educate the public and bring attention to the negative impacts of animal agriculture.

20

The China Study

In 2011, "The China Study" was published, which helped to popularize the idea of a whole-foods, plant-based diet for health. The book, written by T. Colin Campbell and his son Thomas M. Campbell II, presents the findings of a 20-year study conducted by T. Colin Campbell in China, which examined the link between diet and disease. The study, known as the China-Cornell-Oxford Project, is considered to be one of the most comprehensive studies on nutrition ever conducted.

"The China Study" argues that a whole-foods, plant-based diet is the optimal diet for human health and can prevent and even reverse many chronic diseases such as cancer, heart disease and diabetes.

The book presents scientific evidence that a diet rich in animal-based products is linked to an increased risk of chronic diseases, while a diet based on whole plant foods is associated with a lower risk of chronic diseases.

The book was widely praised for its comprehensive examination of the relationship between diet and health, and it helped to popularize the idea of a whole-foods, plant-based diet as a means of preventing and reversing chronic diseases.

It also helped to raise awareness about the negative health effects of a diet high in animal-based products and the benefits of a diet based on whole plant foods.

The China Study" has been influential in the plant-based movement, and it's one of the most cited books in the field of nutrition.

It helped to bring attention to the importance of a whole-foods, plant-based diet and its benefits for health, and it influenced many people to adopt a plant-based diet.

"The China Study" also helped to bring attention to the environmental impact of industrial animal agriculture, as it highlighted how the production of animal-based products is a significant contributor to climate change, deforestation, water and air pollution, and other environmental problems.

The book also emphasized the importance of sustainable food systems and the benefits of a plant-based diet for the environment.

The book also emphasized the importance of nutrient-dense plant foods, such as fruits, vegetables, whole grains, legumes, and nuts, and the role they play in maintaining optimal health. This helped to popularize the idea of a whole-foods, plant-based diet, which emphasizes the consumption of minimally processed and unrefined plant foods, as opposed to a vegan or vegetarian diet that may include processed and refined foods

Furthermore, "The China Study" also helped to bring attention to the importance of a plant-based diet in addressing health disparities and reducing healthcare costs. The book highlighted how a plant-based diet can help to reduce the incidence of chronic diseases among low-income communities and communities of color, which are disproportionately affected by these diseases.

In summary, "The China Study" was a groundbreaking book that helped to popularize the idea of a whole-foods, plant-based diet for health, and the environmental benefits of a plant-based diet in 2011.

It emphasized the importance of nutrient-dense plant foods, and highlighted the role of a plant-based diet in addressing health disparities and reducing healthcare costs.

It helped to raise awareness about the negative health and environmental effects of a diet high in animal-based products, and the benefits of a diet based on whole plant foods.

21

Cowspiracy

In 2013, the documentary film "Cowspiracy: The Sustainability Secret" was released, which helped to bring attention to the environmental impact of animal agriculture. The film, which was directed by Kip Andersen and Keegan Kuhn, examines the impact of animal agriculture on the environment and the role it plays in climate change, deforestation, water and air pollution, and other environmental problems.

The film presents evidence that animal agriculture is one of the leading causes of environmental destruction, and argues that the environmental impact of animal agriculture is not being adequately addressed by environmental organizations.

The film also exposes the lack of transparency and the lack of action from the government and the environmental organizations regarding this issue.

"Cowspiracy" was widely praised for its ability to bring attention to the environmental impact of animal agriculture and for its ability to educate the public on the issue.

The film was successful in raising awareness about the environmental impact of animal agriculture and the importance of sustainable and plant-based diets.

"Cowspiracy" was widely praised for its ability to bring attention to the environmental impact of animal agriculture and for its ability to educate the public on the issue.

The film was successful in raising awareness about the environmental impact of animal agriculture and the importance of sustainable and plant-based diets.

"Cowspiracy" also helped to bring attention to the fact that animal agriculture is responsible for a significant portion of greenhouse gas emissions, deforestation, water and air pollution, and other environmental problems.

The film presented evidence that animal agriculture is a leading cause of climate change and that it contributes to deforestation, loss of biodiversity, and soil erosion.

The film also highlighted the inefficiency of animal agriculture in terms of water usage and land use. It showed how animal agriculture requires significantly more water and land than plant-based agriculture, and how it contributes to water scarcity and land degradation.

The film's release also helped to inspire individuals and organizations to take action on the environmental impact of animal agriculture.

Many people who watched the film were moved by the information it presented and decided to adopt a vegan lifestyle as a result. Additionally, it also helped to push for more sustainable and plant-based food options, as well as for more transparency and action from the government and environmental organizations on this issue.

"Cowspiracy" was a groundbreaking documentary film that helped to bring attention to the environmental impact of animal agriculture in 2013. The film exposed the negative impact of animal agriculture on the environment, and highlighted the inefficiency of animal agriculture in terms of water usage and land use.

It helped to further popularize the vegan lifestyle, raise awareness about sustainable and ethical food choices, and inspired individuals and organizations to take action on the environmental impact of animal agriculture.

22

Veganuary

The Veganuary campaign is an annual event that encourages people to try a vegan diet for the month of January. The campaign was started in 2014 by two friends, Jane Land and Matthew Glover, in the UK, with the goal of encouraging people to try a vegan diet for the month of January and to raise awareness about the benefits of a plant-based diet.

The campaign provides a range of resources and support to help people make the transition to a vegan diet, including recipes, meal plans, and information about the environmental and ethical benefits of a vegan diet.

The campaign also provides a platform for vegans to connect and share their experiences and support each other throughout the month.

The Veganuary campaign has been widely successful and has grown in popularity over the years.

Since its inception, thousands of people have participated in the campaign, many of whom have continued to follow a vegan diet after the month of January.

The campaign has also helped to raise awareness about veganism and the benefits of a plant-based diet. The campaign has also helped to raise awareness about veganism and the benefits of a plant-based diet.

The campaign has also seen growing participation from businesses and organizations, with many offering special promotions and discounts for Veganuary participants, such as vegan menu options in restaurants, vegan options in supermarkets, and vegan products in stores.

This has helped to make it easier for people to adopt a vegan diet and has contributed to the growing acceptance of veganism in society.

The Veganuary campaign has also had a global reach, with participants from over 150 countries participating in the campaign. This has helped to raise awareness about veganism and the benefits of a plant-based diet on a global scale.

In addition to the annual campaign, Veganuary has also expanded its efforts by creating a year-round initiative, "Veganuary Global Impact" which aims to drive demand for plant-based options and help to create a vegan-friendly world, by working with companies and governments to increase the availability and accessibility of plant-based options, and reduce the environmental impact of animal agriculture.

In summary, The Veganuary campaign has been widely successful since it's begining in 2014, and has grown in popularity over the years. The campaign has helped to raise awareness about veganism and the benefits of a plant-based diet, and has made it easier for people to adopt a vegan diet by providing resources and support.

It has also seen growing participation from businesses and organizations and has had a global reach, contributing to the growing acceptance of veganism in society. Veganuary has also expanded its efforts by creating a year-round initiative, "Veganuary Global Impact" to drive demand for plant-based options and help to create a vegan-friendly world.

23

Pandemic

The COVID-19 pandemic had a significant
impact on veganism and the plant-based food
industry. The pandemic led to changes in
consumer behavior and has affected the way
that people think about their food choices.

One of the main impacts of the pandemic on veganism was the increased demand for plant-based products. As people were forced to spend more time at home and cook their own meals, they began to explore new options for plant-based protein sources.

This led to an increase in sales of plant-based meat alternatives, such as soy-based burgers and sausages, as well as a renewed interest in traditional plant-based foods such as beans, lentils, and chickpeas.

Another impact of the pandemic on veganism was the increased focus on the health benefits of a plant-based diet. As the pandemic highlighted the importance of a strong immune system and overall health, many people began to explore the potential health benefits of a plant-based diet.

This led to a renewed interest in plant-based diets, as well as an increase in research and studies on the health benefits of plant-based diets.

The pandemic also affected the way that people buy and consume plant-based products.

With many restaurants and food service establishments closed or operating at reduced capacity, people turned to online grocery stores and meal delivery services to get their plant-based products. This led to an increase in online sales and home delivery of plant-based products.

The pandemic also affected the supply chain of plant-based products. With many food processing plants closed or operating at reduced capacity, there were disruptions in the supply of plant-based products. This led to shortages of some plant-based products and higher prices for others.

The pandemic also affected the way that people perceive the environmental impact of their food choices. The lockdowns and quarantines caused by the pandemic led to a reduction in the carbon footprint of food systems as people were eating more at home and traveling less.

This led to an increased awareness about the environmental impact of food production and consumption, and many people began to explore the potential environmental benefits of a plant-based diet.

Another impact of the pandemic on veganism was the increased focus on the ethical aspects of food production and consumption.

With many people spending more time at home, they had more time to reflect on the way that their food choices affect animals and the environment.

This led to a renewed interest in the ethical and moral implications of consuming animal products, and many people began to explore the potential ethical benefits of a plant-based diet.

However, it's important to note that the pandemic also had negative effects on veganism, as it affected the livelihoods of many small vegan businesses, some of them were forced to close, and the supply chain of plant-based products faced disruptions leading to shortages and higher prices.

Additionally, the pandemic also led to a shift in the way that people perceive food. With many people losing their jobs or facing financial hardships, food became a source of comfort and security.

This led to an increased interest in comfort foods, which often include animal products, and a decreased interest in healthy or alternative diets. This may have had a negative impact on veganism as some people may have turned to animal-based products as a source of comfort.

Furthermore, the pandemic also had an impact on the education and awareness of veganism. With events and gatherings being cancelled, it became more difficult to spread awareness and educate people about veganism. Additionally, with people spending more time online, there was an increase in misinformation and fake news about veganism and plant-based diets, which could have had a negative impact on the perception of veganism.

Additionally, the pandemic also led to a shift in the way that people perceive food. With many people losing their jobs or facing financial hardships, food became a source of comfort and security. This led to an increased interest in comfort foods, which often include animal products, and a decreased interest in healthy or alternative diets. This may have had a negative impact on veganism as some people may have turned to animal-based products as a source of comfort.

Furthermore, the pandemic also had an impact on the education and awareness of veganism. With events and gatherings being cancelled, it became more difficult to spread awareness and educate people about veganism. Additionally, with people spending more time online, there was an increase in misinformation and fake news about veganism and plant-based diets, which could have had a negative impact on the perception of veganism.

VEGAN HISTORY

A comprehensive look at this history of Veganism